M000019357

How to Survive
OLD AGE

CLIVE WHICHELOW *and* MIKE HASKINS

ILLUSTRATIONS BY IAN BAKER

summersdale

HOW TO SURVIVE OLD AGE

An Hachette UK Company
www.hachette.co.uk

Summersdale Publishers Ltd
Part of Octopus Publishing Group Limited
Carmelite House
50 Victoria Embankment
LONDON
EC4Y 0DZ
UK

www.summersdale.com

Printed and bound in China

ISBN: 978-1-78783-031-8

Substantial discounts on bulk quantities of Summersdale books are available to corporations, professional associations and other organisations. For details contact general enquiries: telephone: +44 (0) 1243 771107 or email: enquiries@summersdale.com.

To...................................

From...................................

Introduction

Coming to terms with old age is a matter of pacing yourself. Don't go racing into it like a bull in a china shop, complaining about young people before you're even 35 yourself, or using phrases such as 'I'm not as young as I used to be', or saying, 'Ooh, that's better!' every time you sit down.

And how old is 'old', anyway? Age is largely in the mind. OK, some of it is in the joints, too, but if you avoid living like a couch potato, you might have a few less twinges as the years pass by. It's better to dance to the sound of castanets than to hear your joints sound like castanets every time you try to dance.

And don't compare yourself to glamorous celebrities. Certain people – no names mentioned – may have 70-year-old bodies, but parts of them look less than a fortnight old: the luxuriant chestnut-coloured hair, the gleaming white teeth, the permanently startled expression of one whose face has been lifted more times than an Olympic barbell. No. Be yourself and wear your lines with pride – you've earned them. And anyway, would a tortoise look as lovely with its wrinkles removed? Of course not – it's all about character.

So, take it slowly, ignore the numbers on your birthday cards and let age do its own thing while you get on with doing yours.

All the best things are old anyway: old masters, vintage wines, golden oldies... You're now part of an elite club. Enjoy!

GOOD AND BAD WAYS TO DEAL WITH THE PROBLEMS OF OLD AGE

PROBLEM	GOOD WAY OF DEALING WITH IT	BAD WAY OF DEALING WITH IT
Becoming forgetful	Learning memory techniques	Tying bits of string round every finger
Not hearing so well	Investing in a discreet hearing aid	Keep telling people to stop mumbling
Road signs being indistinct	Having regular eye tests	Getting out of your car to view them close up
Nodding off in front of the TV	Switching the TV off and going to bed for a good night's sleep	Setting an alarm clock for when it's time to go up to bed
Needing to go to the toilet when you are out	Looking for a public toilet	Relieving yourself in public

CLOTHES THAT WILL MAKE YOU LOOK OLD (MEN)

Cheap supermarket jeans

. . . .

Flat cap

. . . .

A sensible waterproof jacket,
even when it's sunny

. . . .

Humorous T-shirt that has your year of
birth printed on the front in big numbers

CLOTHES THAT WILL MAKE YOU LOOK OLD (WOMEN)

Beige tights that wrinkle around your ankles

. . . .

A brown coat that makes you look like
an enormous chocolate Swiss roll

. . . .

A bra that fastens around your waist

. . . .

Twinset and pearls

SAYINGS THAT WILL MAKE YOU SEEM OLD

'You call *that* music?!'

. . . .

'How do you work this thing?'

. . . .

'It wasn't like this in my day'

. . . .

'I don't know what the world's coming to'

'I can remember when sweets
cost tuppence ha'penny'

. . . .

'I'm sure they're making the print
in the newspapers smaller'

. . . .

'Speak up!'

. . . .

'What's your name again?'

'I REMEMBER
WHEN THIS
HOUSING ESTATE
WAS ALL FIELDS'

WAYS TO AVOID LOOKING OLDER THAN YOU ARE

You don't have to have your glasses
dangling from your neck on a piece of string,
as if you can't be trusted not to lose them

. . . .

Stop calling anyone under 40
'young man' or 'young lady'

. . . .

Choose small inconspicuous hearing
aids rather than stuffing a massive
ear trumpet into each lughole

It is not essential to have
a tartan rug over your
knees when in the car

TELLTALE SIGNS THAT OTHERS BELIEVE YOU HAVE REACHED OLD AGE

They ask you if you need the toilet before embarking on any journey, however short

· · · · · · · · · ·

They ask, 'Is he/she still breathing?' every time you nod off

· · · · · · · · · ·

They buy you a funeral plan for your birthday present

THEY DEFER TO YOUR HISTORICAL KNOWLEDGE OF EVERYTHING FROM THE BIRTH OF ROCK AND ROLL TO THE BATTLE OF HASTINGS

GOOD AND BAD TYPES OF OLD PERSON YOU COULD BE

GOOD	BAD
Twinkly-eyed old flatterer	Wrinkly faced, older and fatter
Still running well, like a vintage car	Veined and slightly smelly like a vintage cheese
Ever youthful and doesn't look a day over 50	Can't believe he/she was ever youthful – doesn't look a day under 150
Still fizzing with energy	Looking in desperate need of recharging

TRICKS TO MAKE YOU SEEM YOUNGER THAN YOU ARE

Denying knowledge of any world event
that took place before your twenties

. . . .

Occasionally leaving your winter
coat at home when you go out
in the middle of summer

. . . .

Making an effort to learn all
the songs in the top ten

Offering your seat to an old person on the bus

WHAT OLD AGE IS AND ISN'T

OLD AGE IS...	OLD AGE ISN'T...
Taking things more slowly	Taking things from shops and blaming it on being confused
Being a source of wisdom for younger people in the family	Being a source of income for younger people in the family
An opportunity to spend time with your loved ones	An opportunity to spend time with your loved ones and point out all their faults
A chance to do all the things you've always wanted to do but haven't had the time	A chance to do all the things you've always wanted to do but were worried about the legal repercussions

BREAKDOWN OF YOUR FINANCIAL OUTGOINGS IN OLD AGE (MEN)

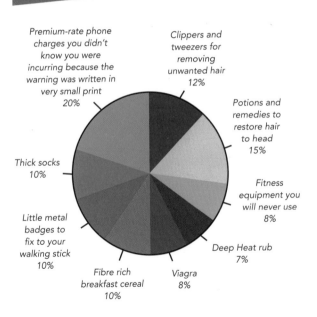

Premium-rate phone charges you didn't know you were incurring because the warning was written in very small print
20%

Clippers and tweezers for removing unwanted hair
12%

Potions and remedies to restore hair to head
15%

Thick socks
10%

Fitness equipment you will never use
8%

Little metal badges to fix to your walking stick
10%

Deep Heat rub
7%

Fibre rich breakfast cereal
10%

Viagra
8%

WAYS IN WHICH DEPICTIONS OF OLD PEOPLE IN FILMS AND ON TV GET IT WRONG

Despite the white hair, they
still look glamorous

. . . .

Younger people actually listen to them

. . . .

They don't gasp with relief every time
they sit down and groan with pain
every time they stand up again

THEY ARE NOT CONSTANTLY BEING PLAGUED BY COLD-CALLERS ON THE PHONE

GOOD AND BAD THINGS ABOUT WRINKLES

GOOD	BAD
They give you character	Regrettably, it's a character from *Planet of the Apes*
Some young people see you as a person with gravitas	Other young people just see you as a person with wrinkles
You can refer to them as laughter lines	An alternative name for them might be 'frown furrows'
They make your face look 'lived in'	Unfortunately, they make your face look 'lived in' by someone who is very untidy

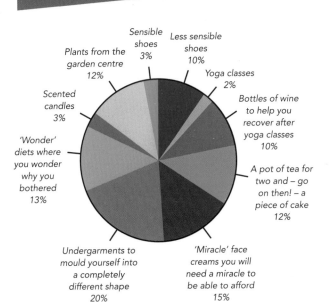

BREAKDOWN OF YOUR FINANCIAL OUTGOINGS IN OLD AGE (WOMEN)

Sensible shoes
3%

Less sensible shoes
10%

Plants from the garden centre
12%

Yoga classes
2%

Scented candles
3%

Bottles of wine to help you recover after yoga classes
10%

'Wonder' diets where you wonder why you bothered
13%

A pot of tea for two and – go on then! – a piece of cake
12%

Undergarments to mould yourself into a completely different shape
20%

'Miracle' face creams you will need a miracle to be able to afford
15%

ADVISABLE AND INADVISABLE LEISURE ACTIVITIES FOR THOSE IN OLD AGE

ADVISABLE	INADVISABLE
The occasional round of golf	A regular round of tequila slammers
Reading a good book	Reading a medical dictionary and self-diagnosing fatal illnesses
Enjoying a day out at a historic property	Enjoying a night out at historic expense
Finding out the secrets of your family history and contacting previously unknown relatives	Finding out the secrets of your family history and contacting previously unknown relatives in order to bribe them

HOW TO SURVIVE MILESTONE BIRTHDAYS

Only have a birthday candle for each decade rather than for each year – you don't want your cake becoming a fire hazard

Remind yourself that at least you won't have to endure another milestone birthday for another ten years

. . . .

Attempting to blow up a balloon for each year you've lived may not just leave you breathless – you might end up using all the available oxygen in your house

Hiring a bouncy castle
for the day may prove
calamitous, especially
if all your guests
are as old as you

WAYS TO KEEP FIT IN EARLY OLD AGE AND EXTREME OLD AGE

EARLY OLD AGE	EXTREME OLD AGE
A bit of light jogging	A bit of memory jogging should be enough
Simple stretching exercises	Just stretching up for the biscuit tin should suffice
A nice long walk	Remembering that nice long walk you went on a few years ago
Swimming a few lengths at the local pool	Floating in a nice, warm bath

CRIMES ONLY THE OLD MIGHT COMMIT

Driving too slowly

. . . .

Loitering without any intent whatsoever

. . . .

Waking the neighbours by going to the toilet too loudly in the middle of the night

. . . .

Offending the public with the curses you utter while bending down or getting back up again

STEERING A SHOPPING TROLLEY WITHOUT DUE CARE AND ATTENTION

GOOD AND BAD THINGS ABOUT LOSING YOUR HAIR

GOOD	BAD
You will save a fortune on shampoo, combs and other hair products	You will now spend just as much on hats
No more dandruff	No more getting mistaken for someone 20 years younger
Many people will respect you more	Many others will just shout, 'Oi, Baldy!'
Some will think you look mature and distinguished	Others may say your 'flyaway hair' has become 'flown-away hair'

THINGS THAT BECOME UNEXPECTEDLY DANGEROUS IN OLD AGE

Eating something toxic because you have trouble reading the label clearly

. . . .

Climbing in and out of the shower

. . . .

Turning your head a little too quickly when trying to see something of interest

*Getting across the
road before the green
man starts flashing*

BREAKDOWN OF HOW YOU WILL SPEND YOUR TIME IN OLD AGE

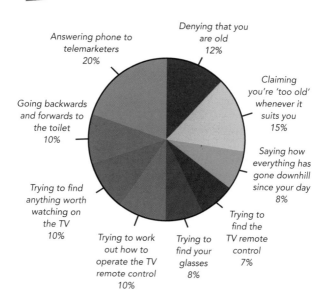

Answering phone to telemarketers
20%

Denying that you are old
12%

Claiming you're 'too old' whenever it suits you
15%

Going backwards and forwards to the toilet
10%

Saying how everything has gone downhill since your day
8%

Trying to find anything worth watching on the TV
10%

Trying to work out how to operate the TV remote control
10%

Trying to find your glasses
8%

Trying to find the TV remote control
7%

THINGS AROUND THE HOUSE THAT MIGHT DATE YOU

Those little covers that go on
the arms of the sofa

• • • • • • • • • •

A collection of LPs, none of which have
been bought since the vinyl revival

• • • • • • • • • •

A leather cover for your TV listings magazine

• • • • • • • • • •

Tea-making facilities next to your bed

VHS and Betamax machines, plus a
row of videocassettes lined up on the
shelf as though they were books

. . . .

A telephone with a rotary dial

. . . .

An instruction booklet on
how to use the internet

ADVISABLE AND INADVISABLE FOODSTUFFS FOR THOSE IN OLD AGE

ADVISABLE	INADVISABLE
Something easy to chew	That rock-hard nougat you loved as a kid
A nice cup of tea several times a day	A large G and T several times a day
A healthy Mediterranean diet of fresh fruit and veg	A serving of chips with everything, inspired by British holidaymakers visiting the Mediterranean
A raw-food diet	Raw sausages because you can't be bothered to heat them up

'OLD' THINGS YOU DON'T HAVE TO DO

Go on an ocean cruise – especially
if you get seasick in a pedalo

· · · · · · · · · ·

Keep your biscuits in a tin with a famous
oil painting printed on the lid

Keep your teeth in a glass by your bedside – this is particularly ill-advised if you don't have dentures!

· · · · · · · · · ·

Have an afternoon nap at exactly the same time every day

WAYS TO SLOW DOWN THE AGING PROCESS

Only celebrate every other birthday

. . . .

Go metric – convert every 12
years of your age to ten!

. . . .

Claim that your birthday
is on 29 February

TRAVEL AT THE SPEED OF LIGHT (DIFFICULT TO ACHIEVE, UNLESS YOU ARE IN A REAL HURRY FOR THE TOILET)

MOBILITY AIDS THAT YOU DO AND DON'T REQUIRE

DO REQUIRE	DON'T REQUIRE
A handrail for getting upstairs	A handrail for getting into your platform boots for a 1970s themed party
A 'grabber' for reaching high shelves	A 'grabber' for getting the attention of a shop assistant
A walk-in bath	A walk-in hot tub in the back garden
A chair with a seat that lifts up to help you stand	A chair with a seat that lifts up and catapults you through the living-room window

ADVICE YOU MAY GET FROM OTHERS (AND CAN SAFELY IGNORE)

Don't let age be a barrier to anything
(with the possible exception of
becoming an Olympic athlete)

. . . .

As long as you've got your health (a bit
of wealth wouldn't go amiss, though)

The important thing is to keep active
(if that's true, why do they make you retire
from work as soon as you get old?)

· · · · · · · · · ·

You're only as old as you feel (if, that
is, you can still feel anything at all)

STRESSFUL – AND EVEN MORE STRESSFUL – WAYS IN WHICH OLD AGE MAY AFFECT YOU

STRESSFUL	EVEN MORE STRESSFUL
You may not be able to dodge traffic so well	You definitely won't be able to dodge childminding duties
You may become more prone to illness	You will become so dosed up with pills and jabs that your doctor won't be able to work out what's wrong with you
You may lose your balance more frequently	You may lose your bank balance to a phone scammer
It may become easier to break a bone	It will be extremely difficult to break into your home if you go out without your keys

WHY YOU'RE NOT REALLY THAT OLD

If you were really that old, you'd
probably be listed by now

. . . .

You can still read the type in
this book – well done!

If you were in line to become
the Pope, you'd still be referred
to as a young candidate

. . . .

You're not really old until you become
fossilised – so just keep moving!

THINGS THAT WILL MAKE YOU FEEL OLDER THAN YOU ARE

The day you qualify for a state pension

. . . .

When people talk loudly in one-syllable words to make sure you can hear and/or understand them

. . . .

When you realise you're looking forward to your next doctor's appointment

When you're
automatically offered
a 'senior discount'
without asking for it

GOOD AND BAD THINGS ABOUT GOING GREY

GOOD	BAD
It's a lot better than losing your hair	If you start dyeing it, you can't really stop
Grey goes with everything in your wardrobe	The only thing it doesn't go with is youth
You can describe yourself as a silver fox	You may look a bit more like a grey seal
You will look distinguished	You can be easily distinguished from anyone young

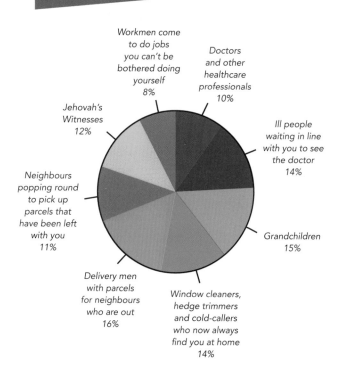

BREAKDOWN OF THOSE YOU WILL SPEND YOUR TIME WITH IN OLD AGE

Workmen come to do jobs you can't be bothered doing yourself 8%

Doctors and other healthcare professionals 10%

Jehovah's Witnesses 12%

Ill people waiting in line with you to see the doctor 14%

Neighbours popping round to pick up parcels that have been left with you 11%

Grandchildren 15%

Delivery men with parcels for neighbours who are out 16%

Window cleaners, hedge trimmers and cold-callers who now always find you at home 14%

GIVEAWAYS THAT YOU'RE TRYING TOO HARD TO LOOK YOUNG

You have 'go faster' stripes
on your walking boots

• • • • • • • • • •

You ask the hairdresser if they
do hair extensions in grey

• • • • • • • • • •

You keep bumping into things because
you refuse to wear glasses

YOU SQUEEZE INTO
TROUSERS SO TIGHT
THAT WHEN YOU
BREAK WIND YOUR
SOCKS INFLATE

THE DIFFERENCE BETWEEN QUITE OLD AND REALLY OLD

QUITE OLD	REALLY OLD
You have trouble getting up the stairs	You have to buy a house without stairs
You have trouble remembering names	You have trouble remembering your own name
The doctor prescribes you several tablets to take every day	You have to ask your doctor to help you get the lids off the bottles
You start suffering from aches and pains	You panic if you suddenly can't feel any aches and pains

DIFFERENT WAYS TO DESCRIBE BEING OLDER

Not old, but vintage –
like a fine wine

. . . .

Just past middle age

. . . .

Not old, just the latest
upgrade of yourself

Not old, but new,
improved and slightly
nearer to perfection

WHY YOU SHOULD BE GLAD YOU'RE NOT YOUNG

You got on the housing ladder while there were still a few rungs near the bottom

• • • • • • • • • •

You don't have to worry about your appearance all the time – mind you, without your glasses you will probably be unable to see your appearance

• • • • • • • • • •

You don't have to spend each night running between nightclubs – instead, you can spend each night running to the toilet

YOU DON'T CARE
WHAT PEOPLE
SAY ABOUT YOU
ON SOCIAL MEDIA
BECAUSE YOU'RE
NOT ON IT

THINGS YOU ONLY REALISE WHEN YOU'RE OLD

Middle age was actually quite young

. . . .

Respected senior citizen is a
contradiction in terms

. . . .

All the things you spent your younger
days worrying about were completely
unimportant – it's when you get old that
you really need to start worrying!

'Older' and 'wiser' don't necessarily go together

ADVISABLE AND INADVISABLE HOLIDAY ACTIVITIES FOR THOSE IN OLD AGE

ADVISABLE	INADVISABLE
Lounging at the hotel pool	Lunging at the hotel staff
Seeing the sights	Looking a sight in your minuscule bathing outfit
Going on a mystery coach tour with a group of other people	Going on a mystery tour on your own in your car because you don't know how to work the satnav
Visiting friends and family who haven't seen you for years	Visiting friends and family who moved to get away from you

HOW TO BE PHILOSOPHICAL ABOUT GETTING OLDER

There's only one thing worse than getting old and that's not getting old

· · · · · · · · ·

I'm still younger than I will be,
so let's make the most of it!

Old age opens up a whole host of new possibilities – unfortunately, you'll be too tired to take advantage of any of them

. . . .

Age is just a number – OK, it's at least a couple of numbers but, taken individually, each one is less than ten

THINGS THAT ARE AND AREN'T WORTH WORRYING ABOUT

WORTH WORRYING ABOUT	NOT WORTH WORRYING ABOUT
Your pension isn't quite as big as you thought it would be	Your waist size isn't quite as small as it used to be
Food doesn't taste quite like it used to	Your musical taste is now more middle of the road than a traffic bollard
You have difficulty remembering the names of family members	You have difficulty remembering the names of characters from TV shows you watched 40 years ago
You can't hear quite so well	You can't hear quite so well when attempting to eavesdrop on your neighbours' arguments

MAKING THE MOST OF THE EFFECTS OF OLD AGE

Hard of hearing – you've now got a cast-iron excuse to ignore anything you don't want to do

. . . .

Wrinkles – get a high-paid job as the 'before' model in skin-cream ads

. . . .

Poor eyesight – you can claim not to have recognised people you want to avoid

MEMORY LOSS –
IT WILL SAVE YOU
A FORTUNE ON
BIRTHDAY CARDS,
PRESENTS, ETC.

PLACES WHERE YOU SHOULD AND SHOULDN'T BE SEEN

SHOULD BE SEEN	SHOULDN'T BE SEEN
Queuing at the post office	Queuing at a nightclub
On a daytime outing	On a dating app
Enjoying a well-earned glass of wine from the supermarket	Enjoying a well-earned bottle of wine by the bins behind the supermarket
Helping out at a local charity shop	Helping yourself at a local charity shop

WHY YOUR NOSTALGIA IS BETTER THAN A YOUNGER PERSON'S

You had the Summer of Love;
they've got global warming

. . . .

You had platform boots; they've
got no-platforming

You remember the day you started paying your mortgage; they remember the day they were first turned down for one

• • • • • • • • • •

You've got a uni sweatshirt and scarf to remind you of your student days; they've got £30,000 of debt

GOOD AND BAD THINGS ABOUT SLOWING DOWN

GOOD	BAD
You'll get help lifting heavy things…	But that help probably won't include your own considerable bulk
You won't get asked to do any more charity fun runs	You'll have to contribute to everyone else's instead
People won't expect you to stay up for an all-night drinking session unless you really want to	They may expect you to stay up and act as their designated driver instead
In the event of an emergency people won't expect you to perform any heroics	In the event of an emergency people may not consider you worth rescuing

TRICKS TO MAKE YOU FEEL YOUNGER THAN YOU ARE

Get one of those fairground mirrors
that make you look taller and thinner

. . . .

Always hang out with older people
who will make you look younger

. . . .

Never look in the mirror while
wearing your glasses

Get yourself a new modern-looking hairstyle – though you might need to get it done using someone else's hair

DON'T PANIC! THE FOLLOWING ARE ALL FAR OLDER THAN YOU

The earth is 4.54 billion years
old – you're not even close

The pyramids were built about 4,600 years ago – however old you are, it is most likely that your birth year doesn't have BC at the end of it!

• • • • • • • • • •

The oldest person who ever lived was over 120 years old – if Guinness World Records hasn't contacted you yet, you must still be a nipper!

THE OLDEST KNOWN BOWHEAD WHALE IS SAID TO HAVE LIVED TO A GRAND OLD AGE OF OVER 200 YEARS – NOT ONLY ARE YOU NOWHERE NEAR THAT, BUT YOU'RE PROBABLY SLIGHTLY SLIMMER AS WELL

If you're interested in finding out more about our books, find us on Facebook at **Summersdale Publishers** and follow us on Twitter at **@Summersdale**.

www.summersdale.com